*I am delighted to recommend
this booklet and the entire
RZIM Critical Questions Series
to you. Written in a popular style and
engaging manner, these booklets are
authored by many notable thinkers and
respected scholars.*

*They are uniquely and specifically
designed for those who have
questions about—and even
difficulties with—belief in God and the
credibility of the Christian faith.*

*Christian believers, too, will greatly
benefit from this series, which will serve
as an important tool to present and
defend their faith in the
marketplace of ideas.*

*I am convinced that these
remarkable booklets will not
disappoint in their readability and in
their persuasiveness for those honestly
seeking answers to life's deepest questions
and to the cultural
confusion around us.*

Rav

1

WHOSE LIFE IS IT ANYWAY?

Assessing Physician-Assisted Suicide

Paul Chamberlain

Paul Chamberlain has a Ph.D. in philosophy from Marquette University (Milwaukee, Wisconsin). He has taught ethics and political philosophy at Trinity Western University (Langley, British Columbia) since 1990. He has written a book on the foundations of ethics, *Can We Be Good Without God?* (InterVarsity Press). More recently, he has written a book on physician-assisted suicide, entitled *Final Wishes: A Cautionary Tale about Death, Dignity, and Physician-assisted Suicide* (InterVarsity Press).

Part of the reason he has taken a special interest in the issues of euthanasia and physician-assisted suicide is that he has watched his own mother suffer from multiple sclerosis over the past thirty years. He has debated a number of proponents of physician-assisted suicide, including prominent Canadian politicians and the executive director of the Hemlock Society.

Paul is married to Gail and is the father of two sons, Tyler and James. He enjoys camping, cycling, and baseball.

ISBN 1-930107-09-9

TOUGH CHOICES: REAL LIFE

❧ Chapter 1 ❧

Cindy was a healthy, athletic woman. She loved aerobics, weight-lifting, and cross-country skiing and was in excellent physical condition. She had a home, a job, and a nine-year-old son. Then tragedy struck. In early 1992, Cindy (not her real name) was diagnosed with ALS. ALS (amiotrophic lateral sclerosis, often referred to as Lou Gehrig's disease) is a progressive, fatal, neuro-muscular disease. It attacks the motor neurons that send electrical signals from the brain to voluntary muscles. As it progresses, it slowly takes away the person's ability to walk, then to talk, and eventually, even to breathe. Without being used, the muscles die, although the brain and all five senses still work. The person wastes away physically, growing weaker until life-support is needed. Most patients eventually die by suffocating or choking. On average, once diagnosed, a person lives two to three years, although some live decades.

Cindy had always been a strong-willed person. After her initial diagnosis, she spent more than $10,000 on naturopaths, acupuncturists, and nutritionists, hoping to prevent the disease from advancing. But by 1993 she was deteriorating seriously. When she finally accepted the reality of ALS, she began to give some thought to her death. Her final days, she realized, would be grim. She would not be able to speak, would have to be fed by tubes, and would breathe on a respirator. She thought about the death that lay ahead and decided, no, she would rather not die that way. If she had to die young, then she wanted to die on her own terms, in her own time.

She came to the decision that she would end her own life when she decided the time was right, when she was no longer enjoying any of the things that gave her pleasure in life. But how does one know when that time comes? In Cindy's words, "I'll just know, and I'll say, 'It's time.'"

Cindy lost the will to live when she was no longer able to hug her son. She knew that soon she would not be able to communicate at all and, in particular, would be unable to express her wish to die. On Saturday, February 12, 1994, Cindy died, on her own terms, at the time of her choosing. Physician-assisted suicide (PAS) was illegal where Cindy lived, but she received one anyway from an unnamed physician who has never been identified. Some of her last words, after being turned down by the courts in her bid to have physician-assisted suicide legalized, were directed at the Supreme Court judges. "I ask you gentlemen," she said, "if I can't give consent to my own death, then whose body is this?"[1]

Bob and Shelley were college students in the '60s. They met and married in 1969. For a while they built careers in retail and hairdressing, but in 1976 they pursued a dream to work together and bought their first business—a family restaurant. For the next eight years they owned and operated a number of restaurants; then in 1984, they took the big step of purchasing the parent-franchise company. Their goal was to reach fifty locations by the age of fifty. They led active lives, working up to ninety hours a week when opening a new restaurant. But they also found time to relax, taking mini-vacations, going for long drives, enjoying numerous summer sports, and bonding with their three grown children—two sons and a daughter. But all this was about to change.

Little signs began to appear that something wasn't quite right with Bob's health. "I had water-skied for twenty-six years," he said, "and then I couldn't hang on to the rope or get out of the water. I just thought I must be out of shape." He had difficulty holding up his arms for activities such as washing the car, blow-drying his hair, or putting on a tie. Shelley noticed he was getting narrow across the shoulders. Then he began having difficulty with his balance and one day, fell down a flight of stairs at work. He could no longer ignore the symptoms and made his first visit to the doctor in January 1997.

A battery of neurological tests followed over the next several months. Bob and Shelley (not their real names) and their children pored over medical journals, searching for answers. They came across a few diseases that fit Bob's symptoms and in their words, "ALS was the one we certainly didn't want." A neurologist delivered the devastating news on August 1, 1997, as Bob, then forty-eight, was stretched out on a hospital bed and Shelley was sitting at the foot. He said, "You have ALS. I'm 99% certain."

How would you respond if you or someone you loved dearly were diagnosed with an illness like ALS? What if you knew that it would result in complete paralysis and, ultimately, would be fatal? Bob and Shelley took the news with disbelief. "We went downstairs and plopped on one of those hospital benches and looked at the world," said Shelley. There were tears. There was fear. There was the painful choice to sell the business they had nurtured and loved for so many years. "I'd never experienced grief like this before," she said.

Bob, too, was overwhelmed by the enormity of it. He grew increasingly weak in his legs and shoulders and soon was walking with a brace and cane, having to give up more of the things he loved. "There was one day last week," Shelley said at one point, reflecting on her own grief, "when I was mowing the lawn and I was crying my eyes out. I looked over at the window and saw Bob standing there watching me doing the things he used to love to do. I can't explain that pain."

Bob and Shelley began dealing with the challenges on a day-to-day basis, but it wasn't easy. They tried not to dwell on the reality of ALS and the frightening path it would take them down. "I don't have the strength for that yet," Shelley said. But sometimes they couldn't escape it. A recent television news program that featured a man in the late stages of the disease was overwhelming. Bob cried for an hour after watching the show.

But none of this has caused Bob and Shelley to look for a way to end Bob's life. Together they draw on their faith and their love for one another to maintain a positive outlook, trying to appreciate the beauty of each day. They see life as a precious gift of God. They believe they are facing this struggle for a reason and that there are lessons to be learned that will become clearer as time goes on. Although it would have been tempting to spend all his remaining energy with his family and on his own interests, Bob is sharing what he has left with other ALS sufferers, trying to raise awareness so more research money is forthcoming. "I hope to make Bob laugh every day of his life," Shelley said. "We rely on the three 'F' words—faith, family, and fun."

Here are two stories of real people who face real suffering; both are true. And they present two diametrically opposed responses to the same agonizing circumstances. But was one response *better* than the other? Should Christians, or anyone concerned about doing the right thing, prefer one response over the other? If so, which one—and why?

WHAT DOES IT ALL MEAN?

❧ Chapter 2 ❧

In recent times there has been an increased demand for physician-assisted suicide (PAS). Why is this so? This is not an easy question, especially when we consider that medical science has given us better pain-control techniques than ever before. Why, with new and better medical help available, are more and more people looking to PAS as the way to end suffering and pain?

It may seem surprising that at least part of the cause of the rising appeal of PAS is this very power of modern medicine itself. The good news is that today we live healthier, longer, more comfortable lives than ever. Our children don't die as often; infant mortality is low in developed countries; and we don't die of infectious diseases like we used to. But modern medicine is a two-edged sword. The downside is that when we do die, it is often of a chronic disease that can bring a long and agonizing death. Diseases like ALS, multiple sclerosis, cancer, emphysema, congestive heart failure, stroke, and AIDS often cause slow and painful deaths. The word is out, and many people have begun looking for a way to avoid that long, drawn-out suffering.

Equally important is the fact that people today want choices. We are a society of people who deeply desire to be in control of our lives. We want the freedom to live and work where we choose; to say what we want to whomever we want; to read, watch, and listen to whatever pleases us; and to come and go at will. We also want to participate in our own medical care more than ever before. We want information and options from our physicians, not merely prescriptions to follow blindly. That sort of so-called "paternalistic medicine" is simply not acceptable anymore to huge numbers of us. And when it comes to the process of dying, this demand for control often leads to a desire to choose when and how we die.

UNDERSTANDING THE TERMS

The Greek term *euthanasia* means literally "good death"—or even "easy death." Over time, however, this term has come to be specifically defined: *the act or failure to act in such a way as to cause the death of a human being for the purpose of relieving suffering.* Because someone in the medical profession is usually involved in these deaths, the term "medicalized killing" is sometimes used to describe this practice.

Traditionally, ethicists have distinguished between *active* and *passive* euthanasia. Active euthanasia is the intentional action to cause the death of a human being in order to relieve suffering. *Passive* euthanasia has been understood as the withholding or withdrawing of life-sustaining treatments in certain conditions resulting in the death of the patient. When thinking of passive euthanasia, it is important to remember that the purpose of medical science has never been to eliminate death altogether, and where the situation is medically hopeless, a decision not to provide or continue extraordinary heroic measures is simply good longstanding medical practice. For this reason, some ethicists contend that the act of allowing a terminally ill person, in the last stages of life, to die a natural death, should not to be called euthanasia in any negative—i.e., morally unjustifiable—sense.[2] This contention has much to commend it.

In drawing these distinctions and evaluating the various kinds of euthanasia, it is important to remember that, morally speaking, intentions matter greatly, and some even prefer to draw the distinctions solely around the intentions. Done this way, providing adequate pain control medication (i.e., morphine) with the intention of easing a person's suffering would not be classified as any kind of euthanasia—even if that medication may hasten the person's death somewhat. On the other hand, if the intention were to bring about the person's death, whether the action were a lethal injection or simply withholding or withdrawing medication, we would have a clear case of euthanasia. Although the idea that "*euthanasia* = the intentional, unjustified hastening of a person's death to ease suffering" is not the standard way of defining these terms (i.e., most ethical discussions use "active" and "passive" euthanasia rather than just "euthanasia"), there is strong merit in defining "euthanasia" this way.

Sometimes one hears the term *mercy killing*. This term is used interchangeably with euthanasia and means the same thing. Because the motives for euthanasia are often compassionate—namely, to end the suffering of another person, the term "mercy killing" is meant to distinguish this form of killing from other forms, which we would call *homicide* or *murder*.

Voluntary euthanasia occurs when euthanasia is carried out at the request of the patient. Against this is a *non-voluntary euthanasia* that happens when the patient is incapable of understanding the choice between life and death. This is different from *involuntary euthanasia*, which is the term used when the patient who is euthanized is capable of consenting to death but does not do so, either because she is not asked or because she is asked but desires to go on living.

A *physician-assisted suicide* occurs when a physician provides the means, method, or both, to a person who desires to end her life but requires help to perform the act. A common form of assistance might be providing a lethal injection of a drug.

There is one last term that one occasionally hears: *rational suicide*. The very existence of this term shows the importance of words and definitions and how they can prepare the mind to accept certain ideas that it might otherwise reject. This term is normally used by those who favor legalizing physician-assisted suicide, and its very use is meant to suggest the possibility that there could be some requests for suicide that are different from the vast majority of suicide requests. Imagine your reaction if you suddenly learned a friend or relative was contemplating suicide. Most of us would react in alarm and would try to intervene with suicide-prevention measures. The desire to die is the result of serious depression or misjudgment or is, in some other way, an irrational desire. At least this is how we would see it. But consider the significance of the term "rational suicide." Even using the term suggests that there could be some requests for suicide which are actually reasonable and which we should take seriously. Terms are important because of their powerful impact on us at a subconscious level.

SEEKING THE RIGHT PATH

Broadly speaking, there are three viewpoints on the spectrum regarding the question of euthanasia or physician-assisted suicide. At one end is the view that *we ought to use every medical means at our disposal to extend every life as long as possible.* Although those who hold this view do so out of a high regard for human life, there are serious reasons why this course of action may be unnecessary and even wrong. With today's medical technology, extending a human life as long as possible runs the risk of using that technology not to heal but merely to prolong the dying process and actually to increase human suffering.

Postponing death as long as possible is not the purpose or proper function of medical science, and we must guard against its being used for that purpose. As stated earlier, it is this very power of modern medicine to prolong an already agonizing dying process that has been a driving force behind the increasing appeal of PAS.

At the other end of the spectrum is the view that *we should use physicians' awesome power over life and death to end intentionally the lives of their patients.* In chapter four we will look at this view closely.

Between these two extremes is a much better middle-ground, *which avoids the extreme of terminating patients' lives, on the one hand, and that of prolonging the dying process, on the other.* This middle view is that we ought to use the medical profession to try to heal when we can. When that is no longer possible, or when the patient requests that we quit trying, we should turn our attention to providing compassionate, palliative care to reduce suffering and pain, increase comfort, deal with the emotional, psychological, and spiritual needs of the dying person, and make the journey with the dying person through the dying process. The goal of this view is to show people who are dying that even in this state, they are valuable, needed, and wanted. Thus, those in the medical field must seek "to cure when possible, to care always, never to kill."[3]

DOES BEING A CHRISTIAN MAKE A DIFFERENCE?

♘ Chapter 3 ♞

One day a young woman put this question to me: "What difference does Christianity make on an issue like PAS or euthanasia? Does the Christian worldview have anything to say about these matters?" It's a fair question, especially when we remember that at the time the Bible was written, today's advanced medical technology did not exist; so of course the ethical questions raised by this technology could not have been specifically addressed in the Bible. How, then, is the Bible or the Christian worldview relevant to this issue?

It is relevant in at least two ways. First, the Christian—or more broadly, the theistic—worldview provides a basis for the most fundamental premise relating to euthanasia—namely, that human life, as the purposeful creation of a loving God, has intrinsic, inherent value.

When creating human beings, God said,

> 'Let us make man in our image, after our likeness . . . . God created man in his image; in the divine image he created him; male and female he created them. (Genesis 1:26, 27)

Human beings have been uniquely created to resemble God in certain limited ways: we are by our very nature rational and moral beings capable of engaging in relationships with God and with one another, in creative enterprises, and in making deeply significant choices. All of this means that human beings—because of their very nature or essence—

ought to be treated with dignity, respect, and compassion—all of them, regardless of their age, race, gender, or ability to function "normally." It is our divinely-given human nature—not how much we can contribute to society, how well we can function physically or mentally, how healthy we are, or how optimistic our prognosis is—that gives us our unique value. This rock-solid principle—that we are humans made in the image of God—is one upon which Christians agree, and we must continually bring this principle to bear upon any discussion of euthanasia or PAS. The principle of human dignity, however, is difficult to ground if God does not exist. Why think that human beings have value if they've been produced by mindless, valueless, impersonal, physical processes? God makes the difference! A non-believer may well believe—and believe strongly—in the dignity of human life (and this is not surprising if we're made in God's image—whether we acknowledge God or not), but he can only do so by *borrowing from* the moral foundations of the Judeo-Christian worldview. Traditionally, this fundamental premise of human dignity has guided medical decision-making, and it should likewise direct all our arguments and discussions on this issue.

And so the question really becomes: *Would we honor and respect human dignity by changing our public policy to give people the right to use the medical profession to help them kill themselves?* In the following chapter we will turn our attention to this important question.

Secondly, another reason being a Christian makes a difference is God's express commandment not to kill wrongfully another human being. The sixth commandment in Exodus 20:13 is traditionally rendered, "Thou shalt not kill."[4] Obviously this instruction is relevant since euthanasia and PAS, by definition, involve one human being killing another. But what exactly, does this verse *mean,* and how does it relate to our question? Is God intending in this command, to rule out all forms of killing of people by other people?

Interestingly, the answer must be no. This cannot be God's intent since in the next few chapters of this very book of the Bible, at least ten capital offenses are set forth—crimes for which *God* calls for punishment by death. It is also worth noting that killing another human being may be legitimate in the case of self-defense or a just war, such as the Allies fighting against the Axis powers to stop their aggression in World War II. Clearly, some forms of killing are permissible in the mind of the same God who said, "Thou shalt not kill." How then should we interpret this sixth commandment? What could God mean by it?

As many have pointed out and many translations make clear, a more accurate rendering of this command is, "Thou shalt not *murder*." This means that rather than ruling out all forms of killing, only *wrongful* killing—*murder*—is being condemned.

While this is important and helpful, it also raises further questions since this command does not spell out *which* kinds and cases of killing are wrongful (i.e., murder) and which are not. In fact, it opens the door to the reality that some kinds of killing are not wrongful, as the next few chapters in the book of Exodus (and the examples of killing in self-defense or in a just war) demonstrate. The pressing question for us is whether PAS and euthanasia are to be included in the definition of murder or could they be permissible forms of killing?

The defenders of PAS, both those who respect the sixth commandment as the Word of God and those who don't, argue that since the motives behind PAS are not malicious, but rather are *compassionate* (namely, to relieve suffering), this kind of killing is different from homicide or murder and is therefore permissible. This is a highly significant claim, and one that we will evaluate in the next chapter along with other reasons for regarding PAS as permissible killing.

While compassionate motives are obviously different from malicious ones, we should make clear at this point that none of the cases of permissible killing set out in the Scriptures involves the killing of a dying person to end that person's suffering. Furthermore, we should not forget the point of the sixth commandment which is to uphold the value of human life and to warn against ending it without some powerfully overriding justification. God has laid out a number of such justifications, as we have noted. As the good Creator and Giver of all life, it is His just prerogative to do so. God gives life as a kind gift, and He is not under obligation to sustain our lives well into retirement age! As human beings, however, we should proceed with great caution in seeking to justify other kinds of permissible killing than those which God has already set out.

The question we must face is the following: Is there any sound justification for PAS? Can we uphold the value of human life *and* support a practice like PAS? It is time to examine the reasons why some say *yes*.

TO LEGALIZE OR NOT TO LEGALIZE?

*Responding to the Case for
Physician-Assisted Suicide*

❧ Chapter 4 ❧

Maybe you've wondered how anyone could be in favor of PAS. Isn't it murder, and isn't murder wrong? Everyone knows that. It's why we have laws against murder, manslaughter, and a host of other actions that would harm or kill humans. How is it, then, that people who support all these laws and value human life highly in other ways can suddenly find PAS to be morally permissible?

Interestingly, most advocates of PAS see no conflict here. In fact, a good number have told me that giving people a choice of when and how they want to die—with the aid of a physician—actually *contributes* to human dignity. But how could it do so? How could the act of ending a human life ever contribute to human dignity? Advocates of legalizing PAS have argued vigorously for their view and have set out their reasons. In recent times a number of these have risen to prominence.

MY BODY, MY CHOICE

Perhaps the most fundamental argument put forward for legalizing PAS is the argument from the right to personal autonomy or self-determination. It usually goes something like this. There are people who are suffering beyond what they wish to endure and who want to end their suffering peacefully and gently. Any person who decides his suffering is too great should have the right to request and receive a PAS. No one has the right to control another person's body or force that person to endure suffering that he does not wish to endure. To do so is an affront to human dignity.

I say this is the most fundamental argument for PAS because at the end of the day, even when supporters of PAS concede other points in this debate, they usually continue to insist that the right to individual autonomy requires that we legalize PAS. People should be given the choice to receive a PAS if they want it. This right, it seems, overpowers all opposing arguments and concerns. It is, in fact, the argument Cindy was alluding to in her statement to the court. If she was not able to choose the time of her own death, then whose body was it? Surely, her body and her life were hers. If not hers, then whose? But if so, then how can we deny that the choice of when and how to end her life must also be hers?

This line of reasoning has great appeal to most Westerners, and especially to those with a strong Libertarian bent, who stress personal liberty—that people should be free to do what they want so long as they do not infringe on the rights of others.[5] But the critical question is: What does this personal-autonomy argument actually *prove*? Not as much as first appears. The fact is that many people want to do many things. Some are good and some bad—not to mention a whole range in between. Would anyone seriously suggest that we give anyone and everyone complete liberty to perform any action at all just so long as they *want* to perform it? What about the person who enjoys drinking and driving or stealing from elderly people or abusing children? These people *want* to do these things. A choice is only as good—or bad or neutral—as the object chosen.

With only a little thought it becomes clear that even for the most ardent Libertarian, it is never enough, when deciding whether or not to make an activity legal, simply to ask whether a person *wants* to do something. One of the most basic principles of liberty set out in any respectable political philosophy class is that individual choice must be limited if political liberty is to be meaningful at all. Without limits, might becomes right, the strongest rule, all liberty is threatened or destroyed, and chaos follows. Legal restrictions are required in order to secure and protect civil liberty. What is sometimes forgotten, however, is that any legal restriction is a restriction on someone's choice whether it concerns driving habits, zoning laws, breaking and entering, and the like.

But perhaps we should pursue the question further. Why, exactly, do we restrict some people's choices? Why not let people do whatever they want to do? At least part of the reason is that some of our actions bring harm to others. In other words, we restrict some choices *not* merely because someone here or there thinks a particular action is immoral or unpleasant; that is seldom argued as sufficient reason to make something illegal. Rather, we formulate laws against all kinds of actions that will harm others or can reasonably be expected to harm others—even if people *want* to carry them out.

But what is the point of PAS? Surely if ever there were a purely private act that brought no harm to others, the act of a physician's assisting a patient to end her life behind the closed doors of a hospital room or private home would be it.

Or would it? Is this characterization of PAS accurate? There is reason to believe that it is overly optimistic. It misses the critical distinction between a *private act*, on the one hand, and a *public policy change*, on the other. This distinction is really at issue here. Legalizing PAS entails changing a public policy, writing a new law to replace a former one. The new law would have to set out what is now legal and available, for whom, under exactly what conditions, and so on. As such, it would affect *far more people* than merely those wanting this new liberty. It would affect everyone whose life circumstances fit the conditions set out in the new law.

Whenever we change public policy, we must at the very least show that the new policy will not harm those directly affected by it and, preferably, that it will bring about more good to them than the policy it is replacing. This, of course, requires that we analyze the effects of the new public policy. What this all means, of course, is that a simple appeal to individual choice or autonomy as *the reason* for implementing any new public policy, including this one, is grossly inadequate.

The relevant kinds of questions then are: What would be the *effects* of changing our public policy to give people the right to use the medical profession to help end their lives? What *possible harm* could come from it? What *burden* might be imposed on others who are affected by this new public policy? Many people are genuinely surprised at the very suggestion that anyone could be harmed or burdened from legalizing PAS. But we should think again.

To see what burden there may be, think carefully of the plight of a person who is elderly, terminally ill, or disabled. Here she is, in the midst of the stress, trauma, and discouragement that comes from facing a terminal illness or a disability. Or perhaps she is a paraplegic or a quadriplegic from a serious accident, living with the fact that she is now a burden and an expense to others—to family, to loved ones, and to care-givers. She needs constant care. She has now become a high-maintenance person. She needs trips to the doctor, the pharmacy, the hospital, and may even need help to be fed or use the toilet. She knows this is causing stress and strain on her loved ones—they're giving up time with family and friends to care for her. They do their best not to reveal any stress, but an elderly or disabled person is not stupid. Occasionally she catches a look of stress on one of their faces and wishes she didn't have to be such a burden. She requires as much care as a one- or two-year-old child, but the difference is that the child will become less dependent with each year.

But that's not all. A person in this position is no longer making the contribution she used to and consequently doesn't often feel needed—something we all long for. She has lost the ability to earn an income and is dependent on others for almost everything. She occasionally finds herself asking what happened to her dignity and sense of self-worth. At times she feels useless. How could she not? This is her life.

Consider the significance for people in these tragic circumstances, of our legalizing PAS. They would be offered the choice to die, and we may wonder what could possibly be wrong with giving them this choice. They don't have to exercise it, but can if they wish. Isn't that the point of giving them a choice?

It is worth noting, however, that contrary to the way we often speak, giving people more choices is not always, invariably, doing them a favor. *Some choices are burdens.* The choice the unfortunate CEO has to make of which 500 employees to lay off is a truly a great burden. So it is with the political leader who has to decide whether or not to send troops into battle, knowing that people will probably die either way. Who among us has not considered a difficult choice facing someone else and uttered the words, "Now there's a choice I'm glad I don't have to make"? Experience teaches us that some choices are burdens, not favors.

And the choice we will have given to the elderly, terminally ill, and the disabled by legalizing PAS will almost certainly impose a devastating burden upon them. By giving them the choice to die, we will have also unwittingly placed upon these vulnerable people—both those who want to die and those who don't—the *added burden of having to justify their own continued existence*, if not to others, at least to themselves. Furthermore, they will have to do this at a time when they feel they are useless, discouraged, and a burden to others. The world will have changed for them because from now on, their own earthly existence involves a choice they must make and may be called upon to justify. People like this may, for instance, be asked why, when other people are choosing PAS (and thus giving up their medical equipment for others and ending the burden and expense on family and society), *they* would like to live on, which, of course, the vast majority would desire.

Consider the words of Peter Kyne, a neuropsychiatrist and palliative-care specialist, commenting on the effects of legalizing PAS upon vulnerable people:

> I know for a fact that people who are dependent upon others, almost universally feel grief and pain over the burden they are to their families. The sense of obligation to exit the situation, if it becomes a legal possibility, will be overwhelming.[6]

This is the harm that could come to these vulnerable citizens by legalizing PAS. Furthermore, discussions one hears from time to time of a possible *duty to die*, or of the potential benefit of harvesting organs for others that could follow from legalizing PAS, would only *add* to the pressure people may feel of having to justify their own continued existence.[7] So this is the first kind of harm that PAS can bring to the terminally ill—*feeling the stress of being a burden to others and the increasing sense of uselessness and the pressure to justify continuing their earthly life.*

Our current laws prohibiting PAS are pillars of protection for vulnerable people. At present, they know they will be kept alive by default. No decision to live need be made because the issue never comes up. No justification is necessary for why one ought to live on or deserves to live on. No discussion with others, or even within one's own mind, is needed. Once PAS is legalized, all that changes.

But couldn't we construct safeguards to protect vulnerable people if PAS is legalized? Couldn't we carefully craft the law in just such a way that we could prevent this abuse? At first blush this may sound reasonable, but again we should think carefully about what we are suggesting. What kind of safeguards could be developed that would protect the elderly and terminally-ill from an inner sense of obligation to choose PAS?

The most commonly suggested safeguards are these: (a) the person must be terminally-ill, experiencing unbearable suffering with no hope of relief; (b) the request for an assisted suicide must be in writing, involving at least two physicians; and (c) the request for suicide must be persistent over time yet be revocable.[8] But it is hard to see how any of these could prevent dependent, vulnerable people from feeling an inner sense of obligation to stop being a burden to their families or caregivers. The problem is not with safeguards. It is that safeguards simply are not designed to prevent this kind of inner sense of obligation. Apart from laws making PAS illegal and, hence, not open to discussion, it is hard to imagine what could.

There is a second form of harm to vulnerable people that could result from legalizing PAS: *the possibility of misdiagnoses that lead patients to request and receive a PAS even though they may not even be terminally ill but think they are.* Every physician knows that medicine is not an exact science, and the possibility of physicians' misdiagnosing their patients is very real. It happens. And because it happens, it allows for the possibility of a physician's actually helping end the life of the "wrong person" if PAS were an available option.

What makes this especially serious is that most requests for suicide come immediately upon patients being diagnosed with a terminal illness or after serious accidents when people are told they are now paraplegics or quadriplegics. *Who wouldn't be highly vulnerable at a time like this?* Devastating news has a way of destroying a person's will to live. Herbert Hendin, Director of the American Foundation for Suicide Prevention, has written:

> In our society right now, even without physicians available to help people die, more individuals, particularly elderly people, kill themselves because they fear and *mistakenly* believe they have cancer, than those who kill themselves and actually have cancer.[9]

Hendin also writes that preoccupation with suicide is greater among those awaiting the results of tests for HIV antibodies than among those who already know they are HIV positive.[10] Think of the plight of these people. They leave their doctors' offices deeply distressed, worried that they have cancer or AIDS—or at least wondering if they might. There is nothing they can do but wait for the test results. Every bruise or stomach pain makes them wonder all over again if they are deathly ill, and yet if there is a misdiagnosis, they aren't seriously ill at all.

The laws prohibiting PAS are there to protect such people. The very possibility that a physician could help a healthy but misdiagnosed and deeply distressed person die is reason enough not to eliminate these pillars of protection. This is why we should seriously question whether a physician's assistance to help end one's life should be available to people who have just heard devastating news.

Interestingly, this form of harm is similar to one often raised by opponents of capital punishment. They argue that the practice of executing criminals creates the possibility of executing an innocent person. This has always been an important consideration in the capital punishment debate and for good reason. Whatever we may think on that issue, over the years innocent people have been executed for crimes they never committed. Others, in countries where capital punishment is not practiced, have been released from life sentences when their innocence has become known. There is little doubt that a similar thing will happen if we legalize PAS. People will ask for PAS who do not even have the diseases they have been told they have.

The third kind of harm almost sure to result from legalizing PAS is that carrying out *this practice would entail making a discriminatory value judgment against the weakest, most vulnerable members of our society, and in the process, would violate the principle of human equality.* We saw earlier that the inherent value and dignity of human life stems not from our powers, potential, or prognosis, but rather from the fact that we are purposeful creations of a loving God who made us in His image. But this means that all members of the human family, *as humans,* share in this intrinsic worth.

This conviction has given rise to the principle of human equality: *all human life is to be valued equally, and we ought not to select one group for lesser treatment than another unless there is some overriding moral justification* (e.g., the waiving of voting rights for incarcerated criminals). It rules out practices such as slavery by asserting that the fact that people are of a certain class or race does not justify devaluing them or treating them worse than other humans. Their shared humanity requires that they be valued and treated with the same respect given to other human beings in similar circumstances. How, then, would legalization of PAS entail a discriminatory value judgment and violate this principle?

To see how, consider precisely *whom* the proponents of legalization have in mind as the beneficiaries of this practice. *For whom* would PAS be intended were it legalized? Would it be for all of us? No, it would not. It would be for the elderly, terminally ill, and perhaps for certain disabled people. The restrictions, or safeguards, suggested by PAS advocates, to be placed around the practice of PAS, invariable try to limit it to these groups of people. Compassion, we are told, requires that we give people in these conditions the option of ending their suffering with suicide assistance. After all, if we were one of them, we may well want that option for ourselves, so we should do for them what we would want done for ourselves.[11]

This sounds compelling until we consider how we might respond if the person who wanted to die were *not* elderly, or terminally ill, or disabled, but rather were able-bodied, healthy, or young—though with deep emotional troubles or in a distressing situation. Should such a person be given suicide assistance to end her life of suffering? "Of course not!" comes the instant reply. "These people need our help in difficult times. They need hope. They need the best suicide prevention measures we can bring them. They have so much to live for."[12] But if compassion requires that we give suicide assistance to the elderly, terminally ill, or disabled when they want to end their lives, then where is our compassion for these able-bodied people who also want to die because of their own painful circumstances? They, too, see their lives as hopeless and as not worth living—to perhaps an even greater degree than the elderly or terminally ill. They too want to end them because of their suffering that they regard as intolerable. If compassion requires us to offer suicide assistance in one case, why not in the other? Let us not forget that if we were in the place of the thirty year-old, able-bodied suicidal person, we would equally want the choice to die.

It looks very much like we have made a value judgment about the worth of lives that are disabled, terminally ill or elderly. *Both* the able-bodied and healthy, on one hand, and the disabled, elderly, and terminally-ill, on the other, are suffering, feel that life is hopeless, and want assistance in dying. However, legalizing PAS with safeguards, which every proponent of legalization calls for, will mean we've decided that while an able-bodied, healthy life is worth fighting for—even to the extent of overriding individual autonomy—a disabled, elderly, or terminally-ill life is not, at least not to the same degree. Somehow, compassion and the right to personal autonomy will have required that we grant suicide assistance to people in this group but not to the other one.

It's hard to avoid the conclusion that, however passionate our statements to the contrary, the disabled, elderly, and terminally-ill human life is valued less, or at least considered less worth fighting for, than the able-bodied, healthy life.

KILLING OR LETTING DIE: ARE THEY MORALLY EQUIVALENT?

Consider the following exchange between Vincent, who favors the legalization of PAS, and William, who does not.

William: Vincent, did I hear you correctly?

Vincent: That depends on what you heard.

William: I heard that you've changed your mind and are now in favor of physician-assisted suicide.

Vincent: You heard correctly. I think it should be legal and available. In fact, I just signed up as a volunteer at a local right-to-die society. We call ourselves "The Good-bye Society."

William: How could you? PAS is killing. You know that's wrong.

Vincent: Oh, really? Well, think about this. You've heard about the woman who was involved in that serious accident and ended up paralyzed from the neck down—Sandy G., they called her. (William nods.) After a couple of years on the respirator, she wanted to die.

William: Yes, I remember.

Vincent: She had nothing to live for anymore, the newspapers said. Everything that gave her pleasure was gone. And do you remember what they did?

William: Sure, they shut off her respirator.

Vincent: That's right, they pulled the plug. A doctor administered morphine, and when she became unconscious, they took her off the respirator.

William: Yes, they let her die. What's the problem?

Vincent: There isn't one so far. But suppose Sandy G. had been suffering from a disease where there was no respirator keeping her alive.

William: Yes.

Vincent: Now imagine she wanted to die. Remember, there is no treatment her doctor could withhold or withdraw to cause her to die, no switch to flip. The only "switch," if you will, would be a lethal dose of morphine or some other injection to end her life painlessly. And would they give it to her? No way. She'd just have to suffer.

William: But that's different.

Vincent: Different? How different?

William: Very different! Can't you see that in one case . . .

Vincent: Look, Will, the important thing is that both these people want to die and both need a doctor's help. But because one happens to be "lucky" enough to have a respirator that can be turned off, she gets the help while the other one does not. It's an inconsistency in the law as far as I'm concerned.

William: How can you say that? What you don't seem to get is that in one case the doctor was merely *letting* the patient die by removing the respirator. In the other, the doctor is *killing* the patient by lethal injection. That sounds like an important difference to me.

Vincent: You call it killing the patient. I call it helping the patient die.

William: But it's still a lethal injection.

Vincent: Of course it is. I just don't happen to see any meaningful difference between *letting* a patient die and *helping* that patient die (or *killing* as you say) in certain cases like this. If you ask me, it's a bunch of meaningless, philosophical hairsplitting. It's hypocrisy.

The argument Vincent has just made is that there is no *moral difference* between killing a person and letting that person die in similar circumstances. In other words, there is no reason to prefer one over the other as a matter of principle. If you believe one of these is morally permissible in a certain circumstance, then you should view the other as also permissible in that circumstance since both are morally equivalent.

This moral equivalence argument is usually stated by pointing out, as Vincent has done, that at the present time, people who are being kept alive by ventilators, respirators, or other life-support systems, may ask to be removed from these systems. They can legally "pull the plug." What is more, these patients need a physician's help to do this. Without that help their deaths could involve painful and needless problems. And they get the help. Physicians shut off life-support systems and administer medication to render their patients unconscious so that death will be painless and humane.

But it makes no sense, Vincent has argued, for a physician to do all of this, but then refuse to help another patient die who likewise is suffering, but simply has no life-support system to shut off. Morally, it is inconsistent. In both cases, a person is suffering, wishing to end life and needing a doctor's help to do so. Furthermore, in both cases the result is the same. The person's life of suffering is over. Even the motives behind the action are said to be the same—namely, to help the person die. The only difference is that in one case there is a switch to shut off while in the other, the only "switch" is a lethal injection. To make a moral distinction between these two actions is seen to be "meaningless, philosophical hairsplitting," as Vincent put it.

Is this reasoning sound? Is there really no moral difference between killing and letting die in similar circumstances? Let us note what has happened here. Vincent has stressed the similarities between certain cases of killing and letting die and drawn this conclusion: because of these similarities, these two kinds of actions are morally equivalent.[13]

Two comments should be made. *First, in emphasizing the similarities, the one key difference that really counts is being overlooked—namely, that when a person is killed by a physician, she dies as the direct result of the actions of the physician.* On the other hand, when a person is *allowed* to die, she does not die as the result of the physician's actions, but *rather as the result of whatever condition she happens to have.* It is the condition, not the physician, which kills. To overlook this difference—despite other similarities—is to overlook the one crucial factor that actually constitutes the difference between killing and letting die—a highly significant difference in making moral judgments.

Secondly, the proponent of the moral-equivalency argument errs on the last similarity—that is, the motives. It is not necessarily true that the motives are the same in cases of killing and letting die. In cases of killing, the motives are clear—*to terminate a person's life.* When a physician administers a lethal injection, his purpose or intention is to end the life of the patient. If, by some chance, the injection were to fail and the patient survive the injection, it would mean the physician's purpose and intentions had been thwarted. The patient is still alive.

When a physician shuts off a respirator, however, the motives may well be merely *to end attempts to heal and let the quite-obvious dying process take its course.* If the person lives on, so be it. The physician's intentions have not been frustrated. It is simply a mistake to say the motives are always the same.

This is important because motives and intentions behind our actions are highly significant in assessing both their morality and legality. It is the difference between one motorist who intentionally steers his car into a group of pedestrians, killing them, and another whose vehicle also careens into the pedestrians, killing them, but only because his brakes malfunctioned and he could not avoid them. In both cases the pedestrians are dead, but we assess (both morally and legally) the actions of the drivers vastly differently.

Most will agree that there are cases in which we are morally justified in letting a person die. In fact, the mere recognition that we all will die someday and that it is futile to try to prevent death forever leads us to accept the fact that when further medical treatment will only *prolong the dying process and increase human suffering,* then there is no obligation to give that treatment. Whether there are also arguments for going the next step, and giving a lethal injection to people (i.e., killing people who would not otherwise die at that time from the conditions they have) is precisely the question at issue. Simply to identify the similarities between killing and letting die, and on this basis assert that there is no moral difference between them, is misguided.

IS THERE A SLIPPERY SLOPE?

The next argument in favor of legalizing PAS is actually a response to one put forward by the opponents of legalization. The argument against legalizing PAS is that it is a practice which, if made legal, would be difficult (and maybe impossible) to contain. Legalizing this practice today would lead to other practices that we all agree would be wrong and unfortunate—such as legalizing PAS for teenagers and for people who are not even terminally ill but just emotionally depressed; euthanizing people who have not requested it; and permitting infanticide.

The response by proponents of legalization is that this slippery-slope argument is wrong-headed. "Admittedly, practices can be, and occasionally are, abused," goes the response. Some drivers ignore the speed limit and a few even drive on the wrong side of the road, but the possibility of abuse of any practice does not automatically constitute a reason to ban it altogether. Instead, we look for ways of dealing with the abuses, of containing them, and in this way guarding our liberties. The possibility of abuses following from legalizing PAS is not said to be a reason to ban that practice either. We can contain these abuses by carefully crafting a law with a set of safeguards, conditions that must be met anytime a PAS is administered, just as we do with all our other liberties. Certain safety measures such as the ones mentioned above are then suggested.[14]

Is this an adequate response to the threat of a slippery slope? Can potential abuses be sufficiently contained such that they do not constitute an argument against legalizing PAS? Is this kind of argument wrong-headed as the proponents of legalization assert?

It is true that certain forms of the slippery slope argument are illegitimate. Most any practice or action can be abused, and the possibility of abuse does not necessarily constitute an argument against every practice. But not all cases are alike. They differ in the seriousness of the potential abuses, the likelihood of these abuses happening, the numbers and kinds of people affected by them, and so on. This all means that there are also different kinds of slippery slope arguments and some are legitimate and should be taken seriously.

In the case of PAS, it is widely agreed that the potential abuses from legalizing it are serious and that the people affected by them are *highly vulnerable*. The only remaining question concerns the *likelihood* of these abuses happening. And it is at this point that, given the nature of PAS, there is good reason to believe the likelihood of abuse would be high. PAS is a practice that would be exceedingly difficult, maybe impossible, to contain. There are two reasons for this.

First of all, in some cases, including PAS, one action does more than simply *invite* the question of pursuing the next action, or *desensitize* people to the seriousness of the next action. Rather, in certain cases, *the reasons we set out for doing one thing actually justify other actions that we have not yet begun to pursue and may not even be thinking of at the time.* This makes a slippery-slope virtually inevitable and unstoppable.

The abuses that have emerged in the Netherlands, where PAS has been legalized, serve as a case in point. In 1991, a fifty-year-old Dutch woman, who was physically healthy but seriously depressed, sought a PAS from her psychiatrist and received one, in violation of the existing legal safeguards. The physician, Dr. Chabot, went to court because of his illegal administering of a PAS. He was eventually exonerated.

We may wonder how he could have been acquitted when he so clearly and indisputably violated the guidelines, but the more important question may be how he could possibly have been convicted. After all, this woman was suffering grievously. She had an abusive alcoholic husband and two sons. Both had died, one through suicide.[15] The woman had decided that her suffering was too great and that she did not want to endure it any longer—the very principle upon which the right to a PAS is based. It states that any person who believes her suffering is too great and no longer wants to endure it should have the right to request and receive a PAS. So she asked for a PAS and got it. Why shouldn't she? The only difference was that her suffering was psychological rather than physical. We may think this is an important difference, but she, her doctor, his lawyer, and ultimately the court did not. Actually, Dr. Chabot's lawyer's very words after the verdict were that the court decision showed that intolerable *psychological* suffering was no different than intolerable *physical* suffering. The fact that this was not the intention of the law permitting PAS or of those who initially argued for it is precisely the point.

The safeguards intended to prevent the move down the slippery slope to other unwanted practices could not stop it because the law making PAS legal rested on the principle that the individual has the right to choose. That is the point of the principle on which PAS is based, and it is always the most fundamental reason given for why this practice ought to be legalized. The legal boundaries in this case conflicted with the fundamental principle of personal autonomy; so they were struck down and rewritten. Courts simply did what courts do. They applied principles and legal precedents consistently.

If this principle were legislated, one wonders how we could deny a PAS to any twenty-five year-old anorexic woman who requests it (which happened in the Netherlands recently—and her request was granted). Or why not grant the request of the aforementioned fifty year-old depressed woman—or any other young person who is physically healthy but deeply depressed and wants to end his suffering with an assisted suicide? The principle says that it is *he*—the one suffering—who decides whether or not his suffering is too great and that he wants an assisted suicide.

What will we tell this person? That his suffering is *not bad enough?* How could we know this? What arrogance on our part to tell him that! Or will we tell him that his suffering is the *wrong kind* of suffering? On what basis would we say that? Or will we say that PAS was *not intended for him* or for the kind of suffering he is experiencing? What does he care? You and I may say all these things and really believe them, but the courts won't because they will do what courts do: interpret principles and precedents consistently. The very reasons for the original principle unwittingly become reasons for granting an assisted suicide to people far beyond the originally intended scope.

After researching the history of PAS in the Netherlands, Herbert Hendin comments on the reality of a slippery slope in that country.

What was intended as an unfortunate necessity in exceptional cases has become a routine way of dealing with serious or terminal illnesses so that doctors are often the first to suggest euthanasia to terminally ill patients.[16]

Elsewhere he says,

Virtually every guideline set up by the Dutch—a voluntary, well-considered, persistent request; intolerable suffering that cannot be relieved; consultation; and reporting of cases—has failed to protect patients or has been modified or violated.[17]

The second reason for thinking that PAS would be impossible to contain concerns *the incentives that exist to move down the slope rather than up it.* These are *incentives*, not reasons or arguments, and they function largely at the subconscious level. There is an economic incentive, which cash-strapped governments everywhere feel, to reduce spending, and healthcare spending is a large part of many government budgets. It is estimated that somewhere between thirty and seventy percent of all healthcare dollars are spent on people in the last sixty to ninety days of their lives. It does not take a great deal of figuring to imagine the savings to cash-strapped governments, which are always looking for ways to cut debts and deficits, if even ten to twenty percent of these people would end their lives before those sixty to ninety days began.

Then, there is *the family incentive.* Those who have gone through the pain of seeing a loved one suffer from a terminal illness, or a long-term debilitating disease, or a serious accident, will know that care-giving family members experience grave burdens and inconveniences. Caring for a person in this condition requires time and energy and is a constant emotional drain. It means visits to the hospital, doctor's office, pharmacy, and so on. It might mean bathing and toileting the loved one. The most saintly person in that situation can be forgiven for having the occasional thought that it would be nice if it were over. Who could blame such a person for sometimes wishing the burden could be lifted? These subconscious incentives, both economic and family, are on the side of sliding down the slope rather than moving up as the likely direction.

COMPASSIONATE KILLING

Rachel (not her real name) was a twelve-year old girl living with cerebral palsy. One day in 1993, her father (a farmer) placed her in his pickup truck, ran a hose from the exhaust pipe to the inside of the vehicle, and started the engine. In thirty minutes, Rachel was dead from carbon monoxide poisoning.[18]

Although many people were deeply troubled by the actions of Rachel's father, there has also been a huge groundswell of sympathy for him. How can this be? Why would anyone sympathize with a man who killed his own daughter? The answer has been loud and clear: He killed her not out of anger or malice, but out of compassion. He did not want his daughter to live on in that condition any longer. This has made all the difference in the way vast numbers of people have judged his actions. And so we must ask: Could killing another human being ever be done out of compassion, and if so, should that change the way we judge the killing? Some have attempted to justify PAS in precisely this way.

The argument goes like this: we must distinguish between two types of killing, (a) killing out of anger, bitterness, or malice, on the one hand, and (b) killing out of compassion, on the other. Whereas we should condemn malicious killing as murder and punish it with a harsh sentence, we ought to treat compassionate killing far differently. It should receive a much lighter sentence and in some cases, no sentence at all. Sometimes the compassionate thing to do is to end a life, and what could be a clearer case of compassionate killing than PAS? It is done out of compassionate motives (i.e., to relieve suffering) and therefore should be seen as morally permissible killing.

What shall we say about this line of reasoning? There is no doubt that compassion is different from anger or malice. We may be tempted to say, therefore, that *killing out of compassion* is also different from *killing out of malice* and should be given a lighter penalty or, in some cases, no penalty at all. But is the presence or absence of compassion the proper criterion by which to measure the rightness or wrongness of killing another human being? If it becomes the criterion for judging killings, at least two serious implications will follow. Let me put them in the form of questions.

First, if compassion becomes the criterion for determining the rightness or wrongness of killing, then *what protection will there be for our most vulnerable citizens, those whose quality of life we tend to view as low?* If we are free, morally and legally, to end the life of a person whose quality of life we regard as so low that it would be compassionate of us to kill him, then it is hard to see what would protect our most vulnerable citizens. *The moment we act out of compassion, it becomes legal to kill them.*

But wouldn't this be limited to those few people who actually *ask* to die? Isn't that what we're talking about with PAS? We may want to limit it this way, but it is critically important to see that if compassion becomes the criterion—a fuzzy, often-subjective, and very pliable one—then no request to die is actually required. All that is required is compassion *in the person doing the killing.* Rachel did not ask to die, but this did not prevent either her father or others from justifying his action on the basis that he acted out of compassion. What is left to protect Rachel and other highly vulnerable people like her?

Secondly, *whose definition of compassion counts?* Who will decide whose compassion is the right kind?

This may not seem difficult or even important until you consider the recent case of a man who killed his ex-lover and her twenty-month-old child. As he put it, after murdering the woman, he killed the child not out of hatred or anger, but out of compassion. He looked into the child's eyes and did not want the child to grow up without a mother.

"How preposterous!" you say, and I agree. But why do we reject this claim as preposterous but not the similar sounding claim by Rachel's father? He, likewise, killed her out of compassion because he did not want her to continue living on in her condition. What's the difference? Eerily, it seems that the difference is that whereas the twenty-month-old child was healthy, Rachel had a quality of life that the rest of us tend to view as so low that it would be compassionate of us to end it. Then we have come full circle to our question of who or what will protect vulnerable people if compassion becomes the criterion by which we judge the rightness or wrongness of killing humans.

ANIMALS

Imagine another conversation between Vincent, the proponent of legalization of PAS and William, the opponent.

William: That's a beautiful dog (commenting to Vincent, who is sitting comfortably in his chair, stroking his black Labrador).

Vincent: Thank you. He's "man's best friend." Maybe that's why we treat dogs better than we treat each other.

William (taken aback, unsure of how to respond): How's that?

Vincent: Think about it. If I were an animal, like this one right here, and I was suffering in pain or had a debilitating disease, they wouldn't let me go on suffering would they?

William: Of course not. That would be inhumane.

Vincent: Ah yes, inhumane. And that's what is so ironic about the way we do things.

William: I, for one, see no irony in treating animals humanely. What's your point?

Vincent: Suppose the one suffering were a human. He'd have pain. He'd lose his independence and probably his dignity too. And yet when he would ask to end his life of suffering, the answer would be no. They wouldn't even do for him what they would do for an animal. Can you believe it? Why can't we treat people at least as well as we treat animals?

This argument made by Vincent is increasingly common. It is that by not legalizing PAS, we end up treating suffering humans worse than we treat suffering animals. When animals in our society suffer greatly, we put them out of their misery. We do not let them linger on and on. Furthermore, we do this because torturing them or letting them continue in their misery would be *inhumane* treatment of animals. But consider the plight of a suffering human in this same society if PAS remains illegal. Whereas an animal's life of suffering will be ended, some humans will have no option but to linger on and on in their suffering even when they go so far as to ask us to end it for them. If animals deserve to be treated with compassion in their suffering, don't humans deserve at least that much?

What can be said to this line of reasoning? Could it be that our moral principles are causing us to deny humans the basic compassion we readily give to animals? On the other hand, could there be reasons why proper treatment of animals does not provide a correct analogy for how we ought to treat humans? Are there considerations to be taken into account when dealing with humans that do not apply to animals?

Imagine homicide detectives being called to a home in a society where people were free to end human suffering by ending human life just as we now end animal suffering. In this home the detectives find a dead person and another person who quickly says to them, "He asked me to do it. He decided life was too great a burden and no longer wanted to live." How are the detectives ever going to begin that investigation? The only person who could confirm or deny this explanation is dead.

This detective example gets at the reasons we have laws prohibiting one person from helping another person die when we do not have the same prohibitions against putting animals down. That is the argument at issue here—namely, that because we end the lives of suffering animals, we should do the same for suffering people. This case highlights at least two reasons why this argument is not persuasive.

First, *we prohibit people from helping other people die to protect us all from being murdered by someone who then uses this "he-asked-me-to-do-it" defense.* After all, as noted above, the only person who could confirm or deny the request for a PAS is now dead and unavailable for further comment. Consider the implications of giving lawyers this defense for clients accused of murder. If such a defense were available, lawyers would be permitted to use it freely. Such recourse would not render them bad or sleazy lawyers. It is a lawyer's job to utilize the reasonable legal means at their disposal to defend their clients, and to whatever degree they used this defense, legal protection for all of us would diminish. To allow one group of people—namely, physicians—to help other people die would make this legal defense available to members of at least this one group. And this undermines the very foundations of medicine, as captured in the Hippocatic Oath, which doctors have traditionally taken: "I will neither give a deadly drug to anybody if asked for it, nor will I make the suggestion to this effect . . . . In purity and holiness I will guard my life and my art." That is, the doctor swears not to kill even when asked to do so.

Secondly, *our laws against helping others die even when they want us to, exist to protect suicidal people from being helped in making the worst decision of their lives in the midst of serious depression and suffering.* Suicidal people need our help to get them through these very difficult periods in their lives. They need protection from people who just might be willing to "help" them make this grave mistake.

The point is that there are reasons for not allowing us to help other people die. The fact that we put animals down does not necessarily mean we ought to do the same for humans. We need more reasons for helping suffering humans die than simply the fact that we help suffering animals die. Perhaps we could even distinguish between what is *humane* and what is *human*, as medical ethicist Leon Kass urges. It is precisely because animals are not *human* that we treat them "humanely" and "put them out of their misery." But being "inhumane" to a person does not imply that we are being "inhuman":

> We put dumb animals to sleep because they do not know that they are dying, because they can make nothing of their misery or mortality, and, therefore, because they cannot live deliberately—i.e., humanly—in the face of their own suffering and dying. They cannot live out a fitting end. Compassion for their weakness and dumbness is our only appropriate emotion, and given our responsibility for their care and well-being, we do the only humane thing we can. But when a conscious human being asks us for death, by that very action he displays the presence of something that precludes our regarding him as a dumb animal. Humanity is owed humanity, not humaneness.[19]

Someone may respond and say, "The *conscious* suffering person may be able to make sense of his suffering, but if he is unconscious or comatose, he cannot make sense of it. Should he not be 'put out of his misery' with a lethal injection?" This question has shifted the issue: the one who is no longer conscious is no longer "suffering," thereby eliminating the purported need to "put him out of his misery." Perhaps it is *our* misery that we're really concerned about.

The ultimate issue, however, is that humans are not animals; there is an ultimate and essential distinction between them: animals do not possess God's likeness and image. So the human is to be bolstered *in the face of death*, not bolstered *into* death.

Now is this detective example really like PAS for a suffering person? Couldn't we carefully craft a law permitting PAS that requires that the person's suffering and wish to die be verified, that physicians and not merely "friends" are involved, that a physician could not use this he-asked-me-to-do-it defense when no such request had been made, and so on?

The important question is: What kind of safeguard could ever prevent a person from killing someone who never asked to be killed, and then using this he-asked-me-to-do-it defense? The surest protection would come from requiring that the request to die be in writing. But this requirement has its own serious difficulties. It would almost certainly be among the first safeguards to be struck down, as it has been in the Netherlands, because it would immediately be seen to *discriminate against* elderly, ill, or disabled people who are unable to write but happen to desire a PAS. Beyond that, this requirement provides no protection for the person who *changes his mind* after stating his request to die in writing, and decides not to go through with the PAS.

Furthermore, not only are all safeguards continually subject to change, as we have noted, but adherence to them also needs to be verified somehow. Due to the nature of medical practice and the private relationship between physicians and their patients, this is not always a simple matter. One prominent physician described the difficulty this way in his submission to a Senate subcommittee holding hearings on this issue:

> I believe that every safeguard that could be created has weaknesses and is open to failure. We know that what doctors do and say to patients is done behind closed doors and is between the doctor and the patient. In the case of euthanasia, the only witness that could testify that safeguards were or were not followed would be dead. The other witness to the safeguards would be unlikely to testify against him or herself. Legislative safeguards of physician-assisted suicide protect the doctor against prosecution, not the patient or the public. I believe that it is my duty as a physician, and a duty of my profession, to tell the public how difficult it would be to monitor and police any safeguards.[20]

This statement points out the extreme limitations of safeguards. It also makes the highly interesting assertion that the *actual* function of safeguards would be radically different from their stated purpose. Rather than protecting *patients* from abuse, they would actually protect physicians who may violate safeguards, from prosecution. While making it legal for the *physician* to end the person's life according to certain safeguards, they provide no mechanism for knowing whether or not the safeguards were followed. As pointed out earlier, the only person able to contest the physician's claim to have followed the safeguards is now dead.

To allow physicians to help other human beings die when they ask for such help would be to destroy the walls of protection for those who have illnesses or disabilities, or who for any other reason become suicidal, and to replace them with a set of shifting safeguards and a legal system that now has a new "he-asked-me-to-do-it" defense in its arsenal (favoring physicians over patients).

Botched Suicides

Vincent: I can see that something is bothering you about physician-assisted suicide.

William: You're a genius.

Vincent: Actually, you make it pretty obvious. What I'd like to know is what's wrong with helping a person die when he asks for the help? Why are you so opposed to it?

William: Well, for a start, may I remind you that it is wrong for someone to take the life of an innocent person.

Vincent (shaking his head): Boy, do you ever need a reality check.

William: So what am I missing?

Vincent: You're missing the fact that assisted suicides are happening whether you like it or not, and whether we make them legal or not. Friends helping friends die, and not always with the aid of a physician either. Sometimes it's with morphine gained illegally and administered poorly. Sometimes it's a plastic bag or even a pillow. We're talking about overdosing, suffocating, or any other method someone might use to help a friend die.

William (wincing): That's awful! It's appalling! It's dreadful!

Vincent: It's also reality. And would you like to hear the real tragic part about it?

William: Not really, but I think I'm going to.

Vincent: The tragic part is that many of these suicide attempts are botched, often with horrific results. I heard of one case where the person . . .

William (interrupting): Okay! Okay! I think I've heard enough. And your solution is. . . .?

Vincent: The solution is simple. Legalize physician-assisted suicide so we can put a stop to these hidden secretive tragedies. That way we could bring this activity out into the open, regulate it, and be more compassionate about it.

The botched suicide argument in favor of legalizing PAS is akin to what is sometimes termed the back-alley argument for abortion. This argument for abortion is that whether it is legal or not, abortions will occur. Some will be performed by amateurs, and women will be harmed or even die. Therefore, to protect these women, we should make abortion legal and bring this practice out into the open where we can regulate it and show proper compassion. Making abortion illegal would be anti-women.

The botched suicide argument similarly is that assisted suicides are happening and will continue whether PAS is legal or not. The assistance is not always given by a physician. It is "friends helping friends die," as Vincent put it—often with tragic results. In the light of these facts, surely it would be better, whether we agree with PAS or not, to legalize it and bring it out into the open as well, where we could regulate it and make it a more compassionate endeavor.[21]

This argument is unique in that, unlike other arguments for PAS, it does not try to prove that PAS is good or right—merely that it is inevitable and that we will only cause more harm by trying to stop it. Furthermore, this reasoning has intuitive force because it appears to recognize life's harsh realities and deal with them.

But is this argument sound? Perhaps we should ask whether or not we would be willing, or should be willing, to be consistent with the principle this argument is based on. The underlying principle upon which it appears to rest is this: Someone's violating a law and being harmed in the process is a good reason to change that law and make the forbidden practice legal. That way no one would ever have to do it in secret anymore. It would be out in the open, regulated, and safe.

However, what if we were to apply this principle to *other* illegal actions? This is a simple way to test any principle to see whether or not it should be followed. I once read of a would-be thief who broke into a store during the night through the heating ducts and began making his way toward the merchandise area. Soon the ducts were too small and as he was sliding through he got stuck, unable to move either in or out. He began to suffocate and nearly died before the surprised business owner arrived in the morning, heard groans, and called for help. Should we then legalize breaking and entering because, legal or not, it is happening and people are being harmed in the process? Obviously not.

But aren't there differences between a case like this and PAS? Yes, there are differences; there always are. No two such comparisons will ever be identical—nor totally dissimilar. There are always similarities and differences when comparing cases; what is critical is whether the things being compared are similar at the *relevant* points. While there are differences between the case of the would-be burglar and PAS, they are not relevant ones. Which facts *are* relevant? (1) PAS and breaking and entering are both illegal; (2) the laws against both are sometimes violated; and (3) in both cases people sometimes get hurt in the process of violating them. All the other differences don't matter at all since the principle this argument assumes does not pertain to them. Thus applying this principle consistently would mean legalizing a host of presently illegal actions that people sometimes perform and get hurt as they do.

Where there are good reasons for any law, then the fact that someone violates the law and is harmed in the process is never *sufficient* reason to change that law, whether it be a law against breaking and entering, drug trafficking, murder, rape, or PAS. Interestingly, the flipside of this is also true. If there are no good reasons for making or keeping something illegal, then we don't even need the botched-suicide argument to set aside that law. *It shouldn't have been there in the first place!* As far as I can tell, the botched-suicide argument serves no useful purpose. It is both unpersuasive and unnecessary.

The Democratic Argument

Vincent: William, it's people like you that scare me.

William: *Me?* Scare *you?* To be honest, I find that rather funny. Why are you scared of people like me?

Vincent: Because you seem willing to impose your views on other people whether or not they agree with you.

William: Oh, and you don't?

Vincent: Absolutely not. No way. I, for one, am unwilling to cast my vote either way on this issue without carefully considering what the people in my society want. After all, it's their country, and they will have to live with whatever decision they have made. And they have made their decision, believe me.

William: That's very democratic of you, Vincent. And what decision have they made?

Vincent (looking dumbfounded): Have you not seen the polls on this issue?

William: Yes, as a matter of fact, I have.

Vincent: Then I hardly need to tell you that virtually all of them show a majority in favor of legalizing PAS. The people want this service available to them regardless of the reasons you, or I, or anyone else may have against it. Now the last time I checked, living in a democracy means the people have the final say.

William (somewhat irritated): Thanks for the lecture, but I think I know what a democracy is. It's a place where you're entitled to hold your opinion on any topic, even this one.

Vincent: Exactly. You have a right to *hold* your own opinion, but not to force it on others who disagree with you.

This argument for PAS is that, regardless of the reasons any of us may have for holding one view or the other on such questions, we ought not to cast our vote either way, or attempt to implement our moral views on these issues without carefully considering the wishes of the people of our society. After all, it is their country, and they will have to live with whatever decisions are made. Various polls and surveys are then pointed to as indicators of the people's wishes, and the results on PAS often indicate that a majority of people want this service to be available.

Given that this is the case, opponents of legalization are told that although they have a right to hold their views on this topic or any other, they do not have a right to force their views on citizens who disagree with them. It is simply wrong, they are told, for a minority of people (or those representing them in government) who do not want this service, to impose their moral values on the populace at large. It is wrong for them to deny the majority a particular service or liberty that it wants to enjoy.

To some, this argument from the nature of democracy seems like the trump card in the PAS debate. After all, we all have our views, but at the end of the day shouldn't the people themselves be able to decide their own fate in matters of morality and social policy? If the majority of people doesn't have this right, then who does? Surely not a minority that simply holds a different view than the majority.

How are we to evaluate this line of reasoning? It has a ring of credibility to the ears of anyone living in a democratic society where, by definition, the majority rules. Elected officials cast votes on the social issues of the day with an eye to the next election.

Two comments should be made about this argument. The first is that *the will of the people is more difficult to discern than it first appears.* Not only is it fickle and changing at the best of times, but the surveys and polls that allegedly report it may yield different results depending upon the knowledge of the people questioned and the wording of the question. The pollster who asks, "Are you in favor of death with dignity for patients in unbearable suffering with no hope of relief?" will garner a different response than the one who asks, "Do you think physicians should ever kill their patients?" This is why a great deal of intense negotiation regularly goes into the process of determining the wording of plebiscites and referenda wherever they are held. And yet the results of polls and surveys on PAS are routinely held up as sure-fire indicators of the will of the people. This difficulty of determining the will of the people is of particular significance with an issue like PAS due to its emotional nature and the vastly different levels of knowledge people have about it.

Secondly, *assuming we can know the wishes of the people, we must ask whether we are prepared to say that this is a reliable method for deciding these issues.* If so, there are far-reaching implications. Not long ago, in Western democracies, a majority of citizens were opposed to women voting. Should we conclude from this fact that at that time it was right and good that women were not permitted to vote? More specifically, are we willing to say that it was right because a majority of people opposed it?

There was also a time in many Western democracies when a majority of citizens believed it was right for black people to be regarded as property and used as slaves. Polls would have registered majority support for this practice as well. In fact, a large part of the economy of some countries had become dependent upon the institution of slavery and when it was attacked by its opponents, its defenders predicted dire consequences that were sure to follow if it was abolished. Are we seriously willing to say that because the majority supported the practice of slavery, it was morally permissible at that time to round up people in Africa, herd them into stench-filled ships, transport them to another country, sell as property those who survived the journey, and treat them as such for the rest of their lives?

To be fair, I must point out that I have never met any proponent of legalization of PAS who also believed that slavery was permissible or morally neutral in its day simply because the majority were in favor of it. It is virtually unanimously considered a shameful blight on our history. But that is precisely the point of this response to the democratic argument for PAS. If the proper approach to determine what should be legalized is following the will of the majority, then, like it or not, we will have no choice but to admit that slavery was at one time permissible and should not have been opposed for precisely the same reason—the majority favored it. If the people at that time had the right to choose their own fate in matters of legalities and social policy and the minority had no right to impose its views on the majority, then we simply have no option but to admit that this heinous treatment of slaves should not have been opposed at that time because of the principle of majoritarianism. But since we would readily admit that slavery should have been opposed back then, despite what the majority may have wanted—and are grateful that it has since been banned in the West, we should admit that (1) the majority can be in gross moral error and therefore may need to be resisted on moral grounds and (2) that the majority vote is not a sufficient guide for making laws and shaping social policy. Since we recognize the problem with "the majority rules" principle when it comes to slavery, we should be alert to similar problems when it comes to PAS.

So the questions we ought to ask about PAS are the same ones that ought to have been asked about slavery. What will be the effect of legalizing this practice upon those most directly affected by it and upon society as a whole? If legalizing PAS would impose a devastating burden on the entire classes of the elderly, terminally ill, and disabled; if it would mean treating the lives of these people as less valuable than others; and if it would risk the possibility that misdiagnosed patients who are not even seriously ill might receive assisted suicides, then the fact that the majority desires it and that it is only a minority that is affected negatively by this practice in no way makes its legalization morally justifiable. In fact, the minority are right to oppose it.

In summary, if I am correct in my evaluations of these arguments for legalizing PAS, then those who favor its legalization will have to seek other arguments if they wish to succeed in making their case.

WHAT, THEN, SHOULD WE DO?

ALTERNATIVES TO PHYSICIAN-ASSISTED SUICIDE

♆ Chapter 5 ♆

At this point we face a question. If PAS is wrong, then what is right? If it is indeed wrong for us to make PAS legal and available to suffering people, then what alternative actions should we take instead? What ought we to do on behalf of people whose suffering and pain are so deep that at least some of them see death as the only way out? Let me make four suggestions.

First, *let us uphold the intrinsic value and dignity of* all *human life.* This is perhaps the most fundamental contribution the Judeo-Christian tradition ought to make to any discussion of euthanasia or PAS. We must gently, but persistently, remind the people of our culture that a person's value and dignity do not depend upon his good health, his capabilities, his condition, his constructive contribution to society, or his positive prognosis. Rather, it stems from his *nature,* from his humanness, from being the purposeful creation of a loving God in whose image he has been made.

But what does it mean to uphold the dignity of all human life? How does one do this? It means, at the very least, that when we hear of a disabled person asking for suicide, we respond to his suicide request in exactly the same way as we would if he were not disabled. We so readily tend to make value distinctions between these two types of people. We look at a person who is disabled, or elderly, or terminally-ill and say to ourselves, "If I were in her shoes, I would probably want the choice to die, so maybe we should give her that same choice now." Yet we would never say any such thing about a young, able-bodied suicidal person. We may see this as compassionate, but many disabled people see this thinking as a direct threat to their own security. And why shouldn't they? One disabled man put it this way recently:

> An *able-bodied* person says, "I want to die." "He is depressed!" is shouted from the rooftops. "He is irrational! Give him suicide prevention help!" The *disabled* person says, "I want to die." "Give him death with dignity" is whispered in the streets.[22]

This double-standard is both subtle and tragic. Let us honor and value all human life equally. We would do well to remind ourselves that the young, healthy, able-bodied person has value not because he is able-bodied or healthy but because he has been created by God in His image. But so have the disabled and elderly and terminally-ill. Our culture needs people who will fly the flag for the intrinsic value and dignity of all human life.

Secondly, let us promote palliative care in our communities for people who are facing death. Sadly, at the present time, many practicing physicians have had little or no training in palliative care. The good news is that interest in this field is beginning to catch on in North America, often at the urging of local citizens. Good palliative care recognizes that we all will die and that it is not the purpose of modern medicine to try to eliminate death. In fact, finding cures and restoring health is only one purpose of medical science. Another is to ease pain and suffering in life's last difficult stages.

This is the special function of palliative care. Rather than seeking to bring healing to people who are facing natural death, its goal is to make the journey through the dying process with a dying person, to increase her comfort, decrease her suffering and pain, and show her that even in this stage of life, she is loved and valued. A great deal of hospice and palliative care is given by volunteers who give many hours to people in their last few weeks or months, tending to their physical, emotional, medical, and spiritual needs. If we are seriously convinced of the inherent value of all human life, then this is one way to demonstrate that conviction.

Thirdly, when you hear elderly, terminally-ill, or disabled people muse about the burden and expense they are to others, about the lack of any contribution they can make, and maybe even about committing suicide (sometimes as a favor to others), recognize that this may actually be a cry for reaffirmation of their own value to somebody. Remember we all deeply desire to be loved and needed by someone. Imagine how you yourself would feel if you were no longer earning anything or contributing much to your circle of family and friends, if you were dependent upon others for all your needs, and if you started wondering if anyone truly needed you or would care if you were gone. Visit vulnerable people! This is critically important. Some of them sit in nursing homes for months without a visit from anyone. Who could blame them for wondering if anyone would miss them if they were gone or for considering PAS as an option? Tell them you love them, you need them, and that you would, indeed, miss them if they were taken from you. Do it enough times to convince them that you really mean it.

I recently spoke with a young man whose elderly grandmother sits in a nursing home and can do very little for herself. He visits her weekly and she once asked him, "Why does God leave me here? Why doesn't He just let me die?" Without skipping a beat the young man looked at his grandmother and said, "God leaves you here because He knows I need you." I'll never forget that answer because in those few words he gave his grandmother an important reason for living. He told her she was needed, and he backed it up by his regular visits. Perhaps most sugnificantly, God can use encouraging comments such as these to help people in the last stages of life to continue to find their hope and security in God and be confident that their earthly work—perhaps of praying for others or cheering and encouraging whomever she can—is not yet finished.

Fourthly, if you know a person who is dying from a painful disease (e.g., some form of cancer), become that person's advocate. Make sure she is not suffering unnecessary pain. It is a wonderful fact that physicians today are able to ease the mose extreme pain suffered by their patients. It is also a fact, however, that many people across North America are dying in severe, unnecessary pain because physicians sometimes undertreat it. There are various reasons for this. Pain is only experienced by the patient. A physician often depends upon the patient to communicate how much pain she is in, and this is not always easy to do. Furthermore, some physicians fear they may run afoul of the law if their pain-control medication could later be shown to have hastened the patient's death, whereas there is no such downside to undertreating pain. Whatever the reasons, it is a travesty that people are dying in intense pain when effective pain-control techniques are available. In fact, as one American doctor recently said, "If pain were uncontrollable, it would be a tragedy; that it is controllable makes it not a tragedy, but a scandal."[23] A Canadian Senator who recently investigated this "scandal" stated wryly that this state of affairs is allowed to continue only because "dead people cannot vote."[24] Vulnerable people need an advocate. They need someone to ask them if they are in pain, and if so, to encourage their physician to intensify the pain treatment.

As we saw at the beginning, Cindy felt there was no way out of her tragic situation but to seek help in ending her life. Bob, on the other hand, has chosen to live on in equally difficult circumstances. Many have made the same choice as Bob: the physicist Stephen Hawking (who has ALS), the Christian writer Joni Eareckson Tada and the actor Christopher Reeves (both quadriplegics), and innumerable others. These people, in their increasing weakness and vulnerability, have chosen a hard path, but individuals like you and me can help them travel it.

Lest we be tempted to think this unimportant, we would do well to remember that showing regard for the needy and marginalized is to honor God, who has made them in His image: "He who is gracious to the needy honors [God]" (Proverbs 14:31). Part of what counts for "true religion" from God's perspective is to "visit orphans and widows in their distress" (James 1:26)—that is, the most vulnerable of society. To treat wrongly those most needful of care is an insult to the God who created them and who is deeply concerned about them.

> Do not rob the poor because he is poor
> Or crush the afflicted [and we could add terminally ill or elderly];
> For the LORD will plead their case . . .
> (Proverbs 22:22-23).

ENDNOTES

❦

[1] From the CBS news program "*Sixty Minutes*". This segment, featuring Sue Rodriguez, aired November 20, 1994 and was entitled "Whose Life Is It Anyway?"

[2] See J. P. Moreland and Norman Geisler, *The Life and Death Debate: Moral Issues of Our Time* (Westport, Conn.: Praeger, 1990), 65; J.P. Moreland, "The Euthanasia Debate: Part I," *Christian Research Journal* (Winter 1992).

[3] "Always to Care, Never to Kill: A Declaration on Euthanasia" (Ramsey Colloquium), *First Things* (February 1992): 46.

[4] As in the King James Version (or Authorized Version) of the Bible.

[5] In addition to this emphasis, Libertarianism stresses personal responsibility, a free-market economy, and non-interventionist foreign policy and free trade. For our discussion, the relevant aspect is *personal liberty or autonomy*.

[6] This statement was made to me in a personal conversation in 1995 with Dr. Peter Kyne, a neuropsychiatrist and palliative-care expert in Vancouver, British Columbia.

Yale Kamisar also says that if euthanasia became a socially approved option, there could be "subtle pressure to request it" (in Herbert Hendin, *Seduced by Death*, 1st ed.[New York: W.W. Norton, 1997], p. 214). See also *When Death Is Sought*, a study carried out and published by the New York State Task Force on Life and the Law, convened by governor Mario Cuomo, published in May 1994. The unanimous recommendations of the task force were that New York laws prohibiting assisted suicide and euthanasia should not be changed. One of the reasons given was that these practices "would be profoundly dangerous for many individuals who are ill and vulnerable." According to the task force, the "risks would be most severe for those who are elderly, poor, socially disadvantaged, or without access to good medical care" (p. ix).

7 See philosopher Margaret P. Battin, "Age-Rationing and the Distribution of Health Care: Is There a Duty to Die?" in *The Moral Life*, eds. Steven Luper-Foy and Curtis Brown (Toronto: Harcourt Brace, 1992), 313-24. In this article Battin assumes a Rawlsian basis for rights and obligations in society and asserts that on this basis, though individuals would not have their lives "discontinued" while in full health, people who are irreversibly ill or of advanced age would have no automatic right to medical care. She says that at a certain point in their illness or age, there would be a "disenfranchisement from care and the expectation that it is time to die" (323). Wesley J. Smith gives a helpful summary of the issue in his book *Forced Exit* (New York: Random House, 1997), 163-79. He includes a quote from former Colorado governor Richard Lamm, who said that old people "have a duty to die and get out of the way" (172).

8 For the view that safeguards could effectively prevent a slippery slope, see Peter Singer, *Practical Ethics* (Cambridge: Cambridge University Press, 1979), 128-29, 140-46. Singer sets out a number of safeguards that have been suggested by voluntary euthanasia societies around the world. Patrick Nowell-Smith in "The Right to Die," in *Contemporary Moral Issues*, ed. Wesley Cragg (Toronto: McGraw-Hill Ryerson, 1992), 7-15, also argues that most serious abuses of legalizing PAS can be "all but eliminated" through proper safeguards. For an opposing view on the effectiveness of these safeguards, see Barry A. Bostrom, "Euthanasia in the Netherlands: A Model for the United States?" *Issues in Law and Medicine* 4, no. 4 (1989): 471-75. Pointing to the Netherlands as an example, Bostrom

describes the changing guidelines from 1973 to 1986 to demonstrate that euthanasia has become more widely practiced and for different reasons than at first intended. For another critique of the effectiveness of safeguards, see Herbert Hendin, *Seduced by Death*, 2nd ed. (New York: W. W. Norton, 1998), 136. He argues that it is impossible to regulate PAS. In his words, "Virtually every guideline set up by the Dutch—a voluntary, well-considered, persistent request; intolerable suffering that cannot be relieved; consultation; and reporting of cases—has failed to protect patients or has been modified or violated."

[9] Dr. Herbert Hendin, director of The American Foundation for Suicide Prevention, in the first edition of his book *Seduced by Death* (New York: W. W. Norton, 1997), 181, cites various studies to show that suicides are being committed today by people who mistakenly believe they have cancer. It is my contention that misdiagnoses lead to this type of mistaken belief about one's health.

[10] Herbert Hendin, *Seduced by Death* 1st ed., 181.

[11] This assertion was made repeatedly by Dr. Faye Girsch, the Executive Director of the Hemlock Society, in a series of public forums in which I participated at six Canadian universities in October 1997. Virtually every proponent of PAS with whom I've ever interacted seriously on this issue has also voiced this same contention.

[12] This exact response was made to me in a public forum when I put this question to a proponent of legalization in June 1995.

[13] The argument that there is no meaningful moral distinction between killing and letting die in similar circumstances is made forcefully by James Rachels in "Euthanasia, Killing, and Letting Die," in *Ethical Issues Relating to Life and Death*, ed. John Ladd (Oxford: Oxford University Press, 1979), 146-61. In this article, Rachels introduces his famous "Smith and Jones" example to illustrate that killing and

letting die are equally reprehensible if the surrounding circumstances are the same. Furthermore, Peter Singer argues in *Rethinking Life and Death* (New York: St. Martin's, 1994), 155-56, that patients would very likely benefit if the distinction between killing and letting die were dropped. A well-known response to Rachels has been made by Thomas D. Sullivan in "Active and Passive Euthanasia: An Impertinent Distinction?" *Human Life Review* 3, no. 3 (1977): 40-46. Two other critiques of Rachels' position are made by J. P. Moreland in "James Rachels and the Active Euthanasia Debate," reprinted in *Do the Right Thing*, ed. Francis J. Beckwith (Sudbury, Mass.: Jones and Bartlett, 1996), 239-46, and by Tom L. Beauchamp in "A Reply to Rachels on Active and Passive Euthanasia," reprinted in *Contemporary Moral Problems*, ed. James E. White (New York: West, 1991), 107-15.

[14] Hendin, Herbert. *Seduced by Death*, 2nd ed. , 136. Peter Singer has set out a number of safeguards that have been suggested by right-to-die societies around the world. These include (1) the patient being diagnosed by two doctors as suffering from an incurable illness expected to cause severe distress or the loss of rational faculties; (2) at least thirty days before the proposed act of euthanasia, and in the presence of two independent witnesses, the patient makes a written request for euthanasia in the event of the situation described in (1) occurring; (3) allowing only a doctor to administer euthanasia and making sure that the patient still wished the declaration to be acted upon; and (4) the patient's declaration could be revoked at any time.

[15] "Killing the Psychic Pain," *Time*, July 4, 1994, 55. This case was explored by Herbert Hendin, who traveled to the Netherlands and interviewed Dr. Chabot, the psychiatrist who administered the physician-assisted suicide. In *Seduced by Death*, 2nd ed., 63-64, 76-87, Hendin provides a more complete description of the process leading to her

death. See also Wesley Smith, *Forced Exit*, 104-5, for another description of the case.

[16] From *Seduced by Death*, 1st ed., 182.

[17] From *Seduced by Death*, 2nd ed., 136.

[18] *National Post*, June 15, 2000.

[19] Leon R. Kass, "Death With Dignity & the Sanctity of Life," *Commentary* (March 1990): 42.

[20] This was part of a presentation made by Dr. Jim Lane, the President of the British Columbia Medical Association, before a Canadian Senate subcommittee, which conducted hearings on euthanasia and physician-assisted suicide on 26 September 1994 (14:26).

[21] This argument is made by Russel Ogden in "When the Sick Request Death: Palliative Care and Euthanasia—A Continuum of Care?" *Journal of Palliative Care* 10, no. 2 (1994): 82-85. In this article Ogden includes a few accounts of botched suicide attempts that he discovered in his research in the AIDS community. For a critique of the botched-suicide argument, see physician H. Robert Pankratz, "The Person in Community: An Examination of Euthanasia," 16-17. This was part of a brief to the Canadian Senate Committee on Euthanasia and Assisted Suicide presented by Canadian Physicians for Life on August 29, 1994.

[22] This was written in an e-mail correspondence I received from Mark Pickup, a victim of multiple sclerosis and anti-euthanasia advocate.

[23] *San Francisco Chronicle*, May 16, 2000.

[24] See Senator Sharon Carstairs' website: http://www.sen.parl.gc.ca/scarstairs/index-e.htm.

SUGGESTED FURTHER READING

❧

Chamberlain, Paul. *Final Wishes: A Cautionary Tale about Death, Dignity, and Physician-Assisted Suicide.* Downers Grove, Ill.: InterVarsity Press, 2000. Written in the form of a fictional story about a medical doctor who is tragically diagnosed with Lou Gehrigs, disease (ALS) and the story of his journey to make this decision. Gives wise and practical counsel on dealing with end-of-life issues.

Smith, Wesley J. *Forced Exit: The Slippery Slope from Assisted Suicide to Legalized Murder.* New York: Random House, 1997. Smith, a lawyer, makes the case that physician-assisted suicide should not be legalized for moral and practical reasons. He claims that "euthanasia is unwise, unethical, and just plain wrong, a social experiment that if implemented will lead to cultural and ethical catastrophe." Instead, we must create a culture of compassion and consider appropriate forms of end-of-life care.

Hendin, Herbert. *Seduced by Death*, 2nd ed. New York: W.W. Norton, 1998. Based on his study of euthanasia in the Netherlands, Hendin argues that in reality, a right to die potentially turns into a duty to die and that pressure from family and medical staff on a patient to opt for euthanasia is very real in the Netherlands. Safeguards against abuse of PAS have uniformly failed. "Patient autonomy" is ultimately "physician autonomy."

Beckwith, Francis. *Do the Right Thing: A Philosophical Dialogue on the Moral and Social Issues of Our Time.* Sudbury, Mass.: Jones and Bartlett, 1999. An anthology of articles on a variety of ethical issues including euthanasia and physician-assisted suicide. Designed for the thoughtful reader to think carefully and critically about important ethical issues.

Moreland, J.P. and Scott Rae. *Body and Soul: Human Nature and the Crisis in Ethics.* Downers Grove, Ill.: InterVarsity Press, 2000. An important defense of humans as spiritual—not merely physical—beings. Investigates how a biblical perpsective on human nature can guide us when dealing with issues such as abortion, euthanasia, cloning, fetal research, and reproductive technologies.

PROJECTED BOOKLETS IN THE RZIM
CRITICAL QUESTIONS SERIES

William Craig, *God, Are You There? Five Reasons God Exists and Three Reasons It Makes a Difference* (available)

Paul Copan, *Is Everything Really Relative? Examining the Assumptions of Relativism and the Culture of* Truth *Decay* (available)

Scott Armstrong, *Who's Shaping My Life? Assessing the Media's Influence on Our Culture*

Darrell Bock, *Can I Trust the Bible? Defending the Bible's Reliability* (available)

David K. Clark and James Beilby, *Why Bother With Truth? Arriving at Knowledge in a Skeptical Society* (available)

Douglas Geivett, *Can a Good God Allow Evil? Making Sense of Suffering*

Klaus Issler, *What Does It Mean To Be Human? Participating in the Game of Life*

Mark Linville, *Is Everything Permitted? Moral Values in a World Without God* (available)

L. T. Jeyachandran *Does the East Have the Answers? Getting Perspective on Eastern Religion and Philosophy*

Stuart McAllister, *Born to Shop? Exposing the Threat of a Consumer Culture*

Paul K. Moser, *Why Doesn't God Make Himself More Obvious? Understanding the God Who Hides and Seeks* (available)

Michael Ramsden, *What's the Point? Finding Meaning and Hope in God*

John Mark Reynolds, *Do the Bible and Science Conflict? Reconciling the Differences*

Ravi Zacharias, *What's So Special About Jesus? Encountering Christ Among the World's Religions*

Keith Pavlischek, *Should God Be Excluded from the Public Square? Understanding the Role of Faith in the Public Life*

Charles Taliaferro, *Does the Idea of God Make Sense? Examining the Coherence of the Divine Attributes* (available)

Paul Chamberlain, *Whose Life is it Anyway? Assessing Physician-Assisted Suicide* (available)

Christopher Wright, *Isn't the God of the Bible Cruel and Vindictive? Understanding Ethical Issues in the Bible*

William Lane Craig, *What Does God Know? Reconciling Divine Foreknowledge and Human Freedom*

Douglas Groothuis, *Lost in Cyberspace? Examining and Overcoming the Dehumanizing Effects of the Computer*

Sam Soloman, *Is Islam the One True Religion? Understanding and Engaging the Muslim Mind.*

Scot McKnight, *Who Was Jesus? Understanding His Identity in Light of Historical Scholarship*

If you have further questions or are in need of additional resources, please contact

Ravi Zacharias International Ministries,
4725 Peachtree Corners Circle, Suite 250,
Norcross, Georgia 30092.

Order line: 800.448.6766
Fax: 770.729.1729
E-mail: rzim@rzim.org
Website on-line ordering: www.rzim.org

RZIM is a ministry founded by Dr. Ravi Zacharias with the goal to reach and challenge those who shape the ideas of a culture with the credibility of the message of Jesus Christ.

If you are interested in obtaining a first-rate philosophical journal written with articles written by leading Christian philosophers, we encourage you to subscribe to *Philosophia Christi*, the journal of the Evangelical Philosophical Society (EPS).

Please contact:

Evangelical Philosophical Society
Biola University
McNally 66
13800 Mirada, CA 90639-0001
philchristi@biola.edu

Copyright © 2002 by Paul Chamberlain.
All rights reserved.

Published by RZIM
Ravi Zacharias International Ministries
4725 Peachtree Corners Circle, Suite 250
Norcross, Georgia 30092
http://www.rzim.org

———————————————————————

Library of Congress Cataloging-in-Publication Data

Chamberlain, Paul, 2002
Whose Life Is It Anyway? Assessing Physician-Assisted Suicide

ISBN 1-930107-09-9

1. Assissted Suicide   2. Terminally Ill
3. Christian Ethics